Keona's
EGG ROLL
STATION

J&K
Style Grill

COPY OUR STYLE, NEVER OUR RESPECT.

KEONA DOOLEY

RESTAURANT   **FOOD TRUCK**

SEASONING & SAUCES

DemDooleys and Associates Inc
dba J&K Style Grill
6557 College Park Sq
Virginia Beach VA 23464
www.JandKStyleGrill.com
jkstylegrill@gmail.com

Photos by
Blanch Perry Photography
Rickie Recardo Photography

An Imprint of Candid Liv

An Imprint of Candid Liv
PO Box 335690
North Las Vegas, NV, 89033
www.candidliv.com

Ordering Information:
Quantity sales. Special discounts are available on quantity purchases by corporations, associations, and others. For details, contact the "Special Sales Department" at the address above.

Keona's Egg Roll Station Keona Dooley. -- 1st Ed
ISBN 978-0-578-91684-2

DEDICATION

One day, I (Kelvin) walked into my late grandmother, Clara's, kitchen and saw my Aunt Sue over the stove, stirring something in a black cast iron pan. She immediately turned and, seeing me looking, said, "Calvin (my name is Calvin), Calvin, I'm making egg roll stuffing. Come taste this."

I'm dedicating the book to Aunt Sue because of her creativity, taste, and excitement. The confidence she had in her food and the many smiles on the faces she fed will always be my inspiration to give people what she gave me. J&K Style Grill, like Aunt Sue, would like you to come into our kitchen to taste some of our favorite styles of egg rolls. We love you, Auntie Sue.

WORDS OF INSPIRATION

Keona, we are proud of you for doing what you love. Hearing your passion when you talk about being creative in the kitchen is amazing. No matter what obstacle you may face chasing your dreams, just remember you have the tenacity to endure it all.

LOVE, UNCLE QUENT AND AUNT OLIVIA

Keona, it is with pleasure that I say: keep living your dreams, following your heart and being a blessing. I am so proud of you!

UNCLE FERNANDO

Keona, keep reaching for the stars and know that we are behind you all the way, helping you keep the course you desire to be on.

LOVE, UNCLE TIM AND AUNT NICOLE

Keke, Uncle Chris is so Godly proud of your achievement in constructing your cookbook. I cannot wait to try some of these recipes. I love you to the moon and back.

TABLE OF CONTENTS

EGG ROLL WRAPPING INSTRUCTIONS

INGREDIENTS

1. Refrigerated Egg Roll Wrappers

2. Filling

3. 1 Teaspoon of Water

Step 1. Lay out your wrapper in a diamond shape. Place 2-3 tablespoons of your mixture in the center.

Step 2. Fold the outer two flaps inward. Make sure the wrapper corners do not touch.

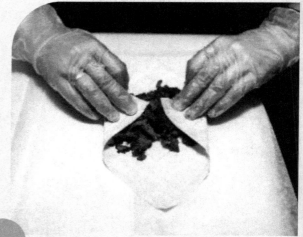

Step 3. Fold the bottom flap upward. Tuck the meat firmly. (If it's too tight can tear the wrapper.)

Step 4. Fold over and continue rolling till the edge until sealed.

Step 5. Secure the edge with water. Remember, too much liquid will make the wrapper soggy.

2

Voila! The finished product! You didn't know it could be so easy, did you?

Cooking Instructions

1. In a medium sized pan, add 2 cups of oil on medium heat (375 degrees).

2. Place the egg rolls in hot oil.

3. Cook each egg roll two and half minutes per side.

4. Remove from pan and let rest for two minutes.

PHILLY STEAK

6oz Philly Steak Meat

½ tsp Minced Garlic

Salt and Pepper to taste

1 oz Peppers, Strips

1 Oz Red Onions, Diced

2 Slices of Cheese

1. Add the steak in a medium saucepan to cook until brown. Add the onion, peppers, and garlic in the same saucepan with steak meat.

2. Chop the meat, onion, peppers and garlic together while cooking.

3. Once it browns, add two slices of cheese. Mix it until it's completely mixed and melted.

4. Remove the steak mixture from saucepan, set it aside to cool, and prepare to roll the mixture into your dough.

5. Let's roll!

OLD SKOOL BEEF TACO

1 tsp Lemon Juice

Pinch of Salt and
Pepper

2tbsp Olive Oil

¼ cup Water

½ lb. 80/20 Beef

½ pkt Taco Seasoning

1 oz. Diced Onions

1 oz. Peppers diced

1 tsp. Minced Garlic

5 oz. Diced Tomatoes

1 tbsp. Cilantro

½ cup Shredded
Cheese

1. In a medium saucepan, simmer the tomato, pepper, onion and garlic in the oil to roast it for seven minutes or until the onions are translucent.

2. Remove the mixture from the skillet, and add it to the blender. Add the water and blend it until it's smooth.

3. In a saucepan, add the meat and the taco seasoning. Cook it until it browns. Pour the mixture into a strainer to separate it from the liquid.

4. Combine the meat mixture and the blended mixture in a sauce pan.

5. Add the shredded cheese and the cilantro to the sauce pan. Mix it well.

6. Let's roll!

PULLED BBQ PORK

2 lb. pulled pork
(store bought)

½ cup Barbeque
(sauce of choice)

½ cup Shredded raw
Cabbage

¼ cup Diced Onions
(sautéed)

2 tbsp Butter

2 tbsp Water

1. In a medium saucepan on medium heat, add the butter, pulled pork, and shredded cabbage.

2. Add 2 tablespoons of water and cover it with a lid. Make sure you stir it constantly so the pork doesn't stick to the pan.

3. Once the cabbage has softened, add the barbecue sauce to the mixture.

4. Remove the mixture from the saucepan and allow it to cool down.

5. Let's roll!

PHILLY CHICKEN

2 lb. Chicken Thighs

1 tbsp Soy Sauce

¼ cup Oil

1 tbsp. Water

2 tbsp. Jerk seasoning dry rub

¼ cup Peppers

¼ cup Red Onions

6 Sliced of Cheese

1. Dice the chicken breast into 1/4 inch cubes.

2. Add the chicken, soy sauce, jerk seasoning, and parsley flakes to a zip locked bag. Shake it to mix it together, and place it in the refrigerator for two hours.

3. Add oil to a large pan on medium heat.

4. Take the marinated chicken out fridge, place it in the pan, and cook it until it's done. It needs to be at an internal temperature of 145 degrees.

5. Add the water and cheese to chicken until the cheese has melted and remove it from the heat.

6. Let's roll!

JERK CHICKEN (GRILLED)

2 lb. Chicken Thighs

1 tbsp Soy Sauce

¼ cup Oil

1 tbsp. Water

2 tbsp. Jerk Seasoning Dry Rub

¼ cup Peppers

¼ cup Red Onions

6 Sliced of Cheese

1. Dice chicken breast into 1/4 inch cubes.

2. Add the chicken, soy sauce, jerk seasoning and parsley flakes to a zip locked bag. Shake it to mix it together, and place it in the fridge for two hours.

3. Add oil to a large large pan on medium heat.

4. Take the marinated chicken out fridge, place it in the pan and cook it until it's done. The internal temperature should be 145 degrees.

5. Add the water and cheese to chicken until the cheese has melted and remove from heat.

6. Let's roll!

BUFFALO CHICKEN

2 lb. Chicken Breast

½ cup Buffalo Sauce

¼ cup Blue Cheese Crumbles

Tbsp Butter

Salt and Black Pepper to Taste

1. Add water, one tablespoon of butter, salt and pepper to a medium sized pot and bring it to a boil.

2. Add the chicken breast and cook it until it's done. The internal temperature should be 165 degrees.

3. Place the cooked chicken on a cutting board. Take a fork and begin to shred the chicken. Add salt and pepper to taste.

4. Discard the water from the pot you used to cook the chicken in the sink. Add the buffalo sauce, butter, and blue cheese to the pot and turn it on medium heat. Stir it to blend the mixture.

5. Add the shredded chicken to pot and mix it all together.

6. Let's roll!

COLLARD GREENS AND SPAM

½ Can of Spam

12oz can Seasoned collards, drained

¼ cup Chopped Red Onions

Tbsp. Vegetable Oil

Salt, Pepper and Red Pepper Flakes to Taste

1. Remove the spam from the can, and slice it down the middle. Take the sliced spam, and cut it into strips.

2. Add oil to a sauté pan and heat it on medium heat until it's hot.

3. Add the onions and cook them until they're translucent.

4. Add the spam strips to the pan. Cook it until you reach your preferred texture.

5. Add the drained collards to the same pan. Add salt, pepper, and red pepper flakes to taste. Once the collards have been cooked and mixed together with the spam, remove the mixture from the pan.

6. Let's roll!

STEAK AND BUTTER POACHED LOBSTER

1 cup Mayonaise

¼ cup lobster Butter

6oz NY Strip Steak (marinated)

1 Lobster Tail Meat, remove from tail

1oz Cream Cheese

8 tbsp Salted Butter

1 cup Mayo

1 tsp Parsley

1 tsp Garlic, Minced (Add Lemon Pepper Seasoning to Taste)

1. Add the mayonnaise and lobster butter together until smooth. Refrigerate it.

2. Mix butter, garlic, and parsley together in a medium pot on medium heat.

3. Chop the lobster and add it to butter. Poach it on low heat for ten minutes.

4. Allow the steak to sit at room temperature for five minutes, upon removing it from the refrigerator. Season the steak with lemon pepper dry seasoning.

5. Cook the steak for six minutes on each side once you add it to the pan. Once it's fully cooked, remove it from the saucepan, and allow it to rest for five minutes.

6. Remove the lobster from the butter. Set the butter aside to make the sauce with.

7. Cut the steak into quarters

8. Mix it all in a bowl, add lobster, cream cheese, and steak.

9. Let's roll!

SHRIMP AND BACON

1 lb. shrimp (peeled and devein)

1 cup. Cabbage

½ cup Shredded Carrots

2 tbsp. Melted Butter

½ tsp. Salt & Pepper

1 tsp. Dry Parsley

4 Strips of Bacon Chopped

1. Chop the bacon and then fry it in a pan. Cook it until it's crispy, and remove it from the saucepan. Keep the bacon grease.

2. Add one tablespoon of butter to the bacon grease on low heat until it's melted.

3. Add the shrimp to the grease and cook it until the shrimp turns pink. Remove the shrimp and chop it up into bite sized pieces on a cutting board.

4. Add the cabbage and carrots to the same pan of bacon grease on medium heat. Add a tablespoon of water and steam it until it's soft. Add the parsley, salt, and pepper. Remove the items from the saucepan.

5. Combine the shrimp, bacon, and cabbage mixture together.

6. Let's roll!

CRAB CAKE

1 lb. Crab Meat

½c Bread Crumbs

½c Parmesan cheese

1 tbsp. Honey Mustard

2 tbsp. Mayo

1 tbsp. Cajun Seasoning

1 tsp. Hot Sauce

1 tbsp. Butter

½ cup Cream Cheese

1 Egg

1. Mix all of the dry ingredients in one bowl.

2. Mix all of the wet ingredients in to a mixture in a second bowl.

3. Combine all of the ingredients until they are incorporated together.

4. Let's roll!

STRAWBERRY CHEESECAKE

3/4 cups frozen strawberry

1 tbsp. Cinnamon

6 tbsp. Sugar

1 Tsp. Vanilla Extract

1:8 oz. Cream Cheese (room temperature)

1 Tbsp. Sour Cream

1. Beat the cream cheese, sour cream, one tablespoon of the sugar, and the vanilla extract together in a bowl.

2. Fold in the sliced frozen strawberries.

3. Combine 1/3 cup of sugar with 1 tablespoon cinnamon in a mixing bowl.

4. Incorporate together.

5. Let's roll!

Acknowledgements

Thank you all for continuing to support me, as a young entrepreneur, and the J&K Style Grill brand. My parents started teaching me business etiquette when I was only nine years old. Under their guidance, I learn, discipline, structure, drive, and love for food. Thanks to my grandparents, aunts, and uncles for keeping me focused and rooted with their many words of encouragement.

Together, with my parents, we would like to say thank you to the following people as well.

We'd like to thank Neal and Beverly Bell for the continued encouragement and love which has inspired us to keep pushing.

We'd like to thank Lamont Wilson for his continued encouragement and reminders that, "God is good and there when we need him."

We'd like to thank Mildred Towns for praying over our restaurant and coming into get her hands dirty when needed. Her favorite egg rolls are the Jerk Chicken Egg Rolls.

Pastor Joyce Graham Butler has always made it her business to speak words of encouragement over our brand. Every word she has spoken has come true. Pastor, here is the cookbook you told us about.

Thank you to the many customers that have come into our business inquiring about how to purchase this book. Thank you for your support. We look forward to continuing to serve you!

Keona Dooley

Connect with us through social media.

jkstylegrill

Visit our website to find more out more information concerning our food truck and restaurant. Also look for our swag, seasoning, and sauces for purchase.

www.JandKStyleGrill.com